A Bowl of Soup, A Crust of Bread, and Thou

Patricia B. Mitchell

Copyright © 1995 by Patricia B. Mitchell.

Published 1995 by the author at the Sims-Mitchell House Bed & Breakfast, 242 Whittle Street SW, P. O. Box 429, Chatham, VA 24531 (telephone 804-432-0595, fax 804-432-0596).

Printed in the U. S. A.
ISBN 0-925117-78-1

Second printing, April 1996

- A Note of Appreciation from the Author -

... To the staff of the Pittsylvania County (Virginia) Public Library for research assistance.

- And to the Reader -

If there is a particular recipe for which you are looking, please write me at the above address and I will try to find it for you. If you have recipes which you would like to share, I would love to receive them.

TABLE OF CONTENTS

INTRODUCTION..1

PART 1: SOUP OF THE DAY..2
    Channel 7 Soup..2
    Dude Mood Soup..3
    Family Night Hamburger Stew...................................3
    Blue Ridge Mountain Chili Soup................................4
    Winter Day Lentil Soup..5
    Epps's Summer Savory Soup....................................6
    Color Me Beautiful Potato Soup................................7
    Grandma's Louisiana Corn Chowder........................7
    Marcelle Bienvenu's Cream of Leek Soup
        with Tasso..8
    Country Farmhouse Soup...9
    Commemorative Voyager Stew..............................10
    Greek Bean Soup (*Fasoladia*).................................10
    "Let's-Stay-Home" Chicken Chowder....................11
    Keyes Lobster Chowder..12
    Louisiana Seafood Gumbo......................................13
    Low-Fat Seafood Gumbo..14
    Provincial Seafood Gumbo......................................15
    Surf 'n' Field Shrimp Chowder.................................15
    Cape Cod Clam Chowder..16
    Tidewater Plantation Oyster Stew..........................17
    Contemporary Crab Bisque....................................18
    She-Crab Soup..19

PART II: WELL-BREAD RECIPES................................19
    Jiffy PB Biscuits..19
    Country Home Scones..20
    Sweet Potato Sherry Scones..................................21
    Lemon-Parsley Biscuits...21
    He-Man Herb Biscuits..22
    Feel-Well Wheat Germ Biscuits...............................23
    Mayonnaise Skillet Bread..23
    Wheat Germ Bread Sticks.......................................24
    Sesame Seed Sticks..24
    Maize 'n' Mozzarella Dodgers..................................25

Teff, Buckwheat, or Kamut Crackers.....................25
Whole Wheat Norwegian Flat Bread
      (Like Crackers)..26
Chatham Carrot Crackers...................................26
Cornfield Biscuits...27
Sweet "Yankee" Corn Bread...............................28
No-Sweetening Yeast Bread................................28
Whole-Grain Goodness Yeast Bread.....................29
Aubrey's Bread...30
Memory Book Colonial Bread.............................31
Yeasty Grits Bread..31
No-Knead Casserole Bread.................................32
Batter-Up Oatmeal Bread (No-Knead)..................32
Dilly Caserole Bread..33
My Honey's French Bread..................................34
Pane Di Campagna (Hearty Country Loaf)............34

NOTES..36

* * * * * * * * * * * * *

INTRODUCTION

I love soup. My mama loathes soup. I used to "fuss" at her, asking how she could say she didn't like soup. -- To me, her attitude seems like claiming that one dislikes vegetables or fruits. Outright rejection of a huge category of foods seems silly, considering the variety available within that category. (Admittedly, I personally do not care for sweet fruit soup, but excluding that type of soup, there are about a million other recipe possibilities . . . .) Anyway, I have given up on trying to convert my mother into a soup lover. Evidently, she associates soup with a grandmother who, after the death of Mom's mother, helped cook for the household. So, to Mom, soup means "no mom," whereas to most of us it means "mama."

I now know a lady who only eats meat and dairy products. She is otherwise a normal, healthy (!), youngish American who simply has never eaten vegetables or fruits. If she can be that way, I guess my mama can just "flat out" not like soup. -- But in both these cases, what a loss of pleasure!

For me, soup is definitely a comfort food. On a chilly day the aroma of a familiar soup wafts around the house, lifting spirits just as surely as the fragrance of Mother's clothes and body make one feel secure; just as certainly as the touch of Mother's hand eases fears and doubts. Mouth-warming, soul-consoling soup seems to whisper "family" and "safety."

Americans consume over 10 billion bowls of soup each year -- January has even been proclaimed National Soup Month[1] -- so obviously I am only one of many soup lovers. Join us "soupers" in ladling up! Add some homemade bread, and you've got it made . . . .

Picture a steaming bowl of soup; some satisfying and substantial bread; and yourself, with mouth watering. -- Now, here are some recipes to turn that mental image into delicious reality!

* * * * * * * * * * * * *

PART 1

SOUP OF THE DAY

"The recording hereinafter of . . . recipes . . . for soup has been a pleasure and a privilege to one who knows what soup can do to hearten people, and how a real interest in soup can cultivate as fine palates as ever the citizens of France have boasted of." [2]

- Sheila Hibben
The National Cookbook: A Kitchen Americana, 1932

CHANNEL 7 SOUP

A few years ago, a film crew came to our house on rather short notice to do a news feature about our bed-and-breakfast and cookbook business. The reporter decided to video my preparation of lunch that day. I was testing the following recipe (which turned out well!).

* * *

2 tbsp. vegetable oil
3 tbsp. flour
3 c. cooked dry limas, and some of their liquid
1 1/2 - 2 c. milk (Non-fat milk is fine.)
1/2 c. canned or fresh tomatoes, chopped
1 (16 oz.) can whole-kernel corn, drained
1/2 c. onion, chopped
2 tbsp. mild green chili peppers, chopped
3/4 tsp. garlic powder
1/2 tsp. *each* salt, chili powder, and celery seeds
1 tbsp. Worcestershire sauce
1 c. Monterey Jack or mozzarella cheese, grated

Slightly heat the oil in a large pot. Blend in the flour. Cook for a few minutes, stirring often. Gradually add 1 1/2 c. milk. Simmer, stirring frequently, until thick. Add the remaining ingredients, except the cheese. Simmer, covered, for 20-30 minutes, stirring occasionally. If the mixture is too thick, add more milk. Just before serving stir in the cheese.

DUDE MOOD SOUP

This Western-style vegetarian soup is a favorite of our little "buckeroos." Both dudes and "dudettes" (as one of the children's friends says) will clean their bowls, and ask for more!

* * *

3 c. cooked red kidney beans or pintos, plus some of their liquid
3 c. cooked black beans (drained and rinsed) or Great Northern beans (undrained)
3 c. canned tomatoes, chopped
3 c. water
2 c. canned or cooked corn, drained
1 c. onion, chopped
1 c. carrots, thinly sliced
2 cloves garlic, minced
2 tbsp. mild green chili peppers, chopped

Combine everything in a big pot. Cook for 1 hour, stirring ever so often. Add hot water if the mixture is too thick.

FAMILY NIGHT HAMBURGER STEW

This good and hearty stew can double as a dinner main course, served over spaghetti noodles and topped with Parmesan cheese.

* * *

1/2 lb. (or more) ground beef, crumbled, cooked, and drained
3 c. undrained canned tomatoes, chopped
2 c. canned tomato sauce
1 can kidney beans, undrained
1/2 c. onion, chopped
1/3 c. celery, chopped
1/4 c. green pepper, chopped
1 (16 oz.) pkg. frozen mixed vegetables

1 tbsp. steak sauce
1 tsp. dry mustard
1/2 tsp. dry basil
Salt and pepper, to suit yourself

Combine all ingredients in a big pot. Bring to a boil, stirring often. Reduce heat, cover, and simmer about 40 minutes, stirring from time to time. Serve in big bowls. (We use "cereal bowls," since we don't happen to own the "proper" large and somewhat shallow soup bowls.)

"Soup is cuisine's kindest course." [3]

BLUE RIDGE MOUNTAIN CHILI SOUP

My college friend, Helen E. Melton of Hillsville, Virginia, is a marvelous cook. She is also generous when it comes to sharing recipes. This "comfort food" soup is one of Helen's recipes. When Helen washes off the potatoes for this good potage she can look right out of her kitchen window at the gently rolling mountains of the Blue Ridge.

* * *

1/2 - 1 lb. ground beef, crumbled, cooked, and drained
2 cans cream of tomato soup
2 cans kidney or pinto beans, or 4 c. home-cooked kidney or pinto beans, plus some of their cooking liquid
2 c. water
1 1/2 c. onions, chopped
2 potatoes, diced
1 or more tsp. chili powder (to your taste)
Salt and pepper

Combine all ingredients in a big pot. Bring to a boil, reduce heat, cover and simmer an hour, stirring occasionally.

"The principal art in composing good rich soup, is so to proportion the several ingredients that the flavor of one shall not predominate over another, and that all the articles of which it is composed, shall form an agreeable whole . . . . In making soups or gravies, gentle stewing or simmering is incomparably the best. It may be remarked, however, that a really good soup can never be made but in a well-closed vessel, although perhaps greater wholesomeness is obtained by an occasional exposure to the air. Soups . . . are much better prepared the day before . . . ." [4]

- Isabella Beeton
The Book of Household Management (1861)

WINTER DAY LENTIL SOUP

As you may know from reading the Bible, the potage for which Esau gave up his birthright was a red lentil stew.

* * *

6 c. water
1 c. dry lentils
2 c. fresh or canned tomatoes, chopped
2 beef bouillon cubes
1 bay leaf
Salt to taste
2 - 3 cloves garlic, minced
1/2 c. *each* potatoes and carrots, diced
1/2 c. *each* onion and celery, chopped

Parmesan cheese

Put all ingredients (except Parmesan cheese) into a large pot. Bring to a boil; then reduce heat, and simmer, covered, for an hour. Stir occasionally. Remove bay leaf before serving. Pass Parmesan cheese to sprinkle on top.

> "Soup is indispensable to the harmony of a formal dinner, and never harms the composition of a brief menu."
>
> - Prosper Montagné, author of
> *Le Grand Livre de la Cuisine*

EPPS'S SUMMER SAVORY SOUP

My accomplished friend Epps Perrow is an artist both at her easel and at the stove.

* * *

3 med. Irish potatoes, diced
2 ribs celery, chopped
2 lg. onions, chopped
Water to cover
1 tbsp. (or more to taste) instant bouillon, chicken flavor
Pepper
Butter (optional)
Dried or fresh summer savory
Milk
Fresh parsley

Put the potatoes, celery, and onion in a pot with water covering the vegetables. Bring to a boil, cover, reduce heat and simmer until the vegetables are tender. At this point add chicken flavoring, pepper, butter, and a little summer savory to season. Stir in enough milk to make the soup the proper consistency. Serve garnished with a sprig or two of fresh parsley if available.[6]

> "Beautiful Soup, so rich and green,
> Waiting in a hot tureen!
> Who for such dainties would not stoop?
> Soup of the evening, beautiful Soup!"[6]
>
> - Lewis Carroll
> *Alice in Wonderland*

COLOR ME BEAUTIFUL POTATO SOUP

3 c. Irish potatoes, cubed
1 c. onion, chopped
1 c. celery, thinly sliced
1 c. carrots, finely diced
2 tbsp. fresh snipped parsley, or 2 tsp. dry parsley
2 tbsp. pimiento, chopped
1 1/2 c. chicken broth (liquid from stewing a chicken, or canned; or use 1 1/2 c. water plus 2 tsp. instant bouillon, chicken flavor)

3 c. milk (I use reconstituted non-fat dry milk.)
1/4 c. flour
1/2 c. milk
Salt and pepper

    Put the first 7 ingredients into a big pot and bring to a boil, stirring often. Reduce heat and cover. Cook until the vegetables are just tender. Add the 3 cups milk and heat thoroughly. In a separate small bowl blend together the flour and 1/2 cup milk, making a thin paste. Gradually stir this into the soup to thicken it. Cook briefly, season to taste with salt and pepper, and serve.

"Only the pure of heart can make a good soup." [7]

- *Ludwig Von Beethoven, 1829*

GRANDMA'S LOUISIANA CORN CHOWDER

    Our adopted Louisiana grandmother, Bea B. Lilly, prepares this "big pot" soup.

* * *

2 med. Irish potatoes, cubed
1 lg. onion, chopped
1 c. celery, chopped

2 lg. carrots, sliced, or 1 can sliced carrots, drained (Reserve liquid.)
1 sm. can tomato sauce
1 sm. can mushrooms
5 cans corn, whole and/or creamed (Drain the whole-kernel corn.)
2 lbs. beef/pork sausage, crumbled, cooked, and drained
1 qt. Half & Half cream
2 pkgs. or cubes beef bouillon dissolved in reserved carrot liquid (or a small amount of water)
1 tbsp. cornstarch
A small amount of milk

In a large pot simmer together the potatoes, onion, celery, carrots, and tomato sauce. (Do not add the carrots at this time if they are canned.) When the vegetables are just tender, add the remaining ingredients except the cornstarch mixture, and simmer 20 minutes or longer. Mix cornstarch and milk and stir into the soup to thicken. Season to taste.

MARCELLE BIENVENU'S CREAM OF LEEK SOUP WITH TASSO

Louisiana native and resident, Marcelle Bienvenu is an outstanding cook and foodwriter. I am proud to call her a special "food friend!"

* * *

8 tbsp. butter (1 stick)
1/2 c. plus 1 tbsp. all-purpose flour
2 - 3 c. coarsely chopped leeks (white and green parts)
1 c. finely chopped tasso (or other smoked ham)
2 qts. chicken broth
6 oz. heavy cream
Salt, pepper, and Tabasco sauce to taste

"First, make the roux. The roux consisting of the flour and butter must cook over a moderate heat with bubbling present 3 to 4 minutes. Otherwise, there will be an uncooked flour taste in the sauce or soup. The roux should be watched and stirred so that it does not turn brown and remains the color of butter for use in the soup. Second, into the hot roux add the leeks and tasso and allow to cook 2 to 3 minutes.

"Third, while stirring slowly, add all the chicken broth to the roux mixture and bring to a simmer, allowing the mixture to simmer 10 minutes or until leeks are tender.

"Fourth, add the heavy cream and return to simmer for 2 to 3 minutes; then season to taste with salt, pepper, and Tabasco.

"Serves 6-8."

Note: Marcelle says that she calls this soup the A-Z soup recipe, because any kind of fresh vegetables can be substituted for the leeks. Also, smoked sausage can be substituted for the tasso.[9]

Voltaire said, "I think more highly of the sunshine and of soup than of all the affairs of the world."[10]

COUNTRY FARMHOUSE SOUP

3 c. cooked red beans
3 c. cooked barley
2 c. cooked corn
6 - 8 c. water, as needed for the desired consistency
1 tbsp. instant bouillon, beef flavor
1 tbsp. dry parsley
1 tbsp. olive oil
3 cloves garlic, minced
Salt and pepper to taste
1/4 lb. summer sausage, diced, or bulk sausage, crumbled, cooked, and drained

Combine all ingredients and simmer together at least 45 minutes.

Louis XIV, King of France, routinely demanded and ate one bowl each of four different kinds of soups at a meal.

COMMEMORATIVE VOYAGER STEW

This is a personal favorite of mine and young son Jonathan.

* * *

1 lb. dry split peas
6 - 8 c. chicken broth
1 c. onion, chopped
1 clove garlic, minced
2 bay leaves
1/2 tsp. salt
1/8 tsp. pepper

Rinse the peas, and then put them in a large pot. Add the chicken broth. (I use the liquid in which I have stewed a chicken. -- I chill the liquid and then remove the hardened chicken fat from the top.) Add the onion, garlic, and bay leaf to the peas and cook covered for an hour or more, adding more broth (or water) if necessary. Stir occasionally. Add salt and pepper. Taste the stew (really more like a soup) and add more salt and pepper, if desired. Remove the bay leaves before serving.

GREEK BEAN SOUP (*FASOLADIA*)

1 lb. Great Northern beans
1 c. onion, chopped
1 c. celery, chopped
1 c. carrots, chopped
4 c. tomatoes, chopped
2 tbsp. olive oil
3 - 4 cloves garlic, minced
1 bay leaf
Crushed red pepper, salt, and pepper to taste
1/2 tsp. oregano

Rinse and sort beans. Cover with water and soak overnight; then bring to a slow boil and cook until the beans are just cooked. Add remaining ingredients and simmer until all ingredients are tender. (Add more water if needed.) Remove bay leaf before serving.

NOTE: The original recipe from the *Nichols Garden Nursery Herbs & Rare Seeds 1993* catalog suggested using Flageolet beans, dry shelled Romanos, or other white beans in this traditional European soup.

"Soup is economical food, and by a little attention may be made good with very small materials." [11]

- Young Housekeeper's Friend, 1846

"LET'S-STAY-HOME" CHICKEN CHOWDER

"Chowder" comes from the French "*chaudière*," or "pot." Chowder usually contains seafood, milk, potatoes, and onions. This winsome soup is a spin-off from that theme.

* * *

1 can cream of chicken soup
3 - 4 c. chicken broth (that in which you cooked the chicken)
2 c. Irish potatoes, diced
2 c. chicken, cooked and chopped
1/4 c. green pepper, chopped
1 (16 oz.) pkg. frozen mixed vegetables
Salt and pepper to taste
1/4 tsp. curry powder

    Combine canned soup and chicken broth in a large pot. (Use more broth if you want a less-thick chowder.) Heat to boiling. Add potatoes. Cover, reduce heat, and cook until the potatoes are tender. Add other ingredients. Simmer, covered, until the mixed vegetables are cooked (about 5-10 minutes). Makes 6 servings. Outstanding accompanied by corn bread!

Note: The Campbell Soup Company would be pleased with my ample use of their canned soups. As you know, opening a can of creamed soup to use as a "base" for a dish is a real short-cut in meal preparation. I'm also indebted to Campbell's for lots of recipe ideas. I found this chowder recipe in a magazine advertisement for Campbell's, and I modified it only a little.

"Could anything be more comforting than looking forward to a big plate of hot soup, ladled forth at table from an ample soup tureen, promising, by its very girth, 'seconds for all?'" [12]

- June Platt
June Platt's Plain and Fancy Cookbook, 1941

KEYES LOBSTER CHOWDER

Frances Parkinson Keyes was a beloved novelist of the earlier part of this century. She wrote, among other things, *Dinner at Antoine's*. She was also an accomplished hostess and wife of a senator. Here is one of her recipes.

* * *

4 (2 lb.) lobsters
1 qt. milk
1 pt. cream
1/4 c. onion, chopped
1 clove garlic, minced
1 tbsp. flour
1/4 c. butter
1 tsp. Worcestershire sauce
Salt and pepper to taste
2 soda [Saltine] crackers

Simmer the lobsters in boiling, salted water for 1 hour; and then split them in half lengthwise. From each half, break off the large claw and attached arm. Remove the meat from these parts, and from the tail section. Reserve the brownish green liver, and in females, the red coral roe. Pull out lungs, stomach, and intestinal pieces and discard. Crush the shells, cover them with one cup boiling water and simmer 10 minutes. Strain this water and combine it with the four cups milk, two cups cream, onion, and garlic. Bring this liquid just to a boil, and then simmer for 30 minutes. Strain. Meanwhile make a smooth paste of the 1 tbsp.

of flour and the butter. Add the lobster livers (and roe). Stir this paste into the liquid in the saucepan. Cut the lobster meat into small pieces and add this, the Worcestershire sauce, and salt and pepper. Simmer in a double boiler for half an hour. Just before serving, stir in the finely crumbled crackers.[13]

"Soup-making is the most important part of good housekeeping...."[14]

- Sheila Hibben
The National Cookbook: A Kitchen Americana, 1932

LOUISIANA SEAFOOD GUMBO

As my readers know, husband Henry and I used to live in New Orleans, so we often have an *envie* (a longing) for Louisiana food -- especially *magnifique* seafood gumbo. There are those like us "for whom nothing is ever as good" as Creole/Cajun food.

* * *

3 lg. tbsp. vegetable oil
3 lg. tbsp. flour
2 lbs. shrimp, peeled and deveined
3 c. okra, chopped
2 large onions, chopped
2 tbsp. vegetable oil
1 can tomatoes
3 cloves garlic, minced
2 qt. water
Salt, black and red pepper
1/2 pt. oysters
1 can crabmeat
Several whole crabs cleaned and their claws
1/2 c. parsley, finely chopped
1/2 c. green onion tops, finely chopped

Rice
Fresh filé

Make a roux of the three spoons oil and flour, stirring constantly until dark brown. Add shrimp to roux and cook for a few minutes. Set aside. Then cook okra and onions in oil. Add tomatoes and garlic when okra is almost done. Cook a few minutes longer, then add water and salt and pepper. Combine shrimp roux mixture with okra mixture and simmer for about 30 minutes. Add oysters, crabmeat, and whole crabs and simmer until crabs are cooked. Add parsley and green onions and simmer another 15-20 minutes. Serve over rice and let each person add fresh filé to their taste.[16]

Note: *Dry* filé powder may be used to flavor and thicken the gumbo. Stir it into the soup just before serving.

LOW-FAT SEAFOOD GUMBO

2 qt. water
1/2 c. oil-free roux* (See below.)
1 tsp. red pepper (You may want to use less.)
2 tbsp. parsley flakes
2 tsp. sodium-free creole seasoning
1 c. green pepper, chopped
1 c. celery, chopped
1 1/2 c. green onions (including tops), chopped
1 lb. shrimp, peeled and deveined
1 lb. (claw) crab meat
1 lb. small raw oysters

Cooked rice

Measure 1-1/2 quarts of water in a 6 quart pan. Bring to a boil. Gradually add 2 cups cold water to oil-free roux,* mixing well to make a smooth paste. Slowly stir in roux mixture to 1-1/2 quarts of boiling water. Add red pepper, parsley flakes, and sodium-free creole seasoning to water. Add green pepper, celery, and green onions. Let mixture simmer for 45 minutes. Add shrimp, crab claw meat, and oysters and let simmer for 30 minutes.

Serve over cooked rice. Serves 12.

*OIL-FREE ROUX: . . . Place about one inch of flour in a black iron pot or baking pan. Place in a 400° F. oven, stirring occasionally with a wooden spoon, until the desired darkness.

Add to sautéed vegetables and stock, then add shrimp, crab, chicken, etc. Or: Bake in oven on dry cookie sheet at 400° F. for 1 1/2 hours. Should be color of light brown flour. Add water to form paste. Store in air-tight container in freezer.[16]

PROVINCIAL SEAFOOD GUMBO

Gumbos can be complex, or relatively easy to prepare. This delicious gumbo is worth waiting for when you order it at the Honfleur Restaurant in the Hôtel Provincial on Chartres Street in New Orleans' French Quarter, or you can make it yourself!

* * *

3 lg. onions, chopped
1 bell (green) pepper, chopped
A small amount of oil or fat
5 lg. crabs, cleaned
3 (16 oz.) pkg. frozen okra
1 lg. can tomato sauce
3 lbs. shrimp, peeled and devined
Garlic powder

Cooked Rice

Fry onions and bell pepper till soft. Add crabs and fry a while (about fifteen minutes) on medium heat. Add okra and fry a while (about twenty minutes or more). Add tomato sauce. Add enough water to make about a gallon of gumbo. Add salt, pepper, and garlic powder, and simmer on low heat about 1 and 1/2 hours. Add raw shrimp and let it come to a boil. Cook about 10 minutes.

Serve on rice.[17]

SURF 'N' FIELD SHRIMP CHOWDER

An old family favorite . . . .

* * *

1 tbsp. vegetable oil
1 - 2 tsp. garlic powder
2 c. onions, chopped

2 or 3 fresh tomatoes, peeled and chopped (or a 16-oz. can of tomatoes)
5 Irish potatoes, diced
1 tsp. salt, or to suit your taste
1/2 tsp. crushed red pepper
1 tsp. chili powder
A few drops of Tabasco sauce or soy sauce
3 c. water
2 c. milk (plus 1/2 c. additional)
1 (3-oz.) pkg. cream cheese
1 lb. shrimp, peeled and deveined
1 1/2 c. fresh, canned, or frozen whole-kernel corn

Heat the oil and add garlic powder, onions, tomatoes, potatoes, salt, crushed red pepper, chili powder, and Tabasco or soy sauce. Stir. Slowly add water and then two cups of milk, stirring occasionally. Bring to a boil, then cover and simmer for 30 minutes.

Meanwhile, beat the cream cheese with the 1/2 cup milk until smooth. When the potatoes are tender, blend in the cream cheese. Add the shrimp and corn, and cook until the shrimp are pink (five or ten minutes). Serve this steaming chowder in big bowls. There is enough for at least six people, and it can be frozen.

A Gulf Coast restaurant proclaims, "Try our clam chowder. It's uncanny."

CAPE COD CLAM CHOWDER

This New England classic will "warm the cockles of your heart."

* * *

1 qt. clams with liquor
1/4 lb. salt pork, diced
2 qt. water
5 med. Irish potatoes, cubed

1 med. onion, chopped
2 c. milk
1 tbsp. butter
Salt and pepper

Discard tough part of clam stomach and neck. Chop remaining part. Fry salt pork. Remove and reserve. Add water, clam liquor, potatoes, and onion to fat; cook 15 minutes. Add clams; cook until clams and potatoes are tender. Add milk and butter; heat, but do not boil. Add salt pork and season to taste. (Canned clams and broth may be used in this recipe.) Serves 8.

TIDEWATER PLANTATION OYSTER STEW

Especially popular at Christmas, oyster stew is so delectable, it should be an all-winter favorite.

* * *

1/4 c. butter
1 pt. oysters and their liquor
Salt and pepper
1/8 tsp. celery salt
1 1/2 c. milk

Melt butter in a saucepan; add oysters and their liquor. Cook over medium heat until hot, stirring often. (Do not overcook.) Add remaining ingredients. Gradually add milk, stirring all the while. Cook over medium heat until oyster edges curl.

"It breathes reassurance, it offers consolation; after a weary day it promotes sociability . . . . There is nothing like a bowl of hot soup, its wisp of aromatic steam teasing the nostrils into quivering anticipation."[18]

- Louis P. DeGouy
The Soup Book (1949)

CONTEMPORARY CRAB BISQUE

Bisque is believed to be French Provençal in origin. It is now sometimes called a "*coulis,*" and is a thick puree made with some crustacean (crayfish, lobster, crab, etc.).

* * *

1 (10 3/4 oz.) can cream of mushroom soup
1 (10 3/4 oz.) can cream of asparagus soup
2 - 3 c. milk (depending upon the consistency you desire)

Heat together. Add:

1 (6 oz.) can crabmeat, drained and flaked
1/4 - 1/3 c. dry white wine or sherry

Serve warm.

I love to eat crabs, but I also find live crabs very interesting creatures to observe. (I even had a pet crab for a while, until a mean cousin poured ice water all over him and killed him. -- It was summertime and the change evidently shocked him to death . . . .)

When we have traveled to Nassau our hotel always had crab races for the guests' enjoyment. A large circle of rope was laid on the beach. We guests each selected a number. A man standing in the center of the circle poured a "herd" of crabs out onto the sand from a cardboard box. Each crab had a number on his back. The crab who crossed the rope and went out of the circle first was the winner. The guest who had that number won a bottle of champagne. We received several bottles over the years. -- Thank you, sweet crabs!

"The Spanish have an old proverb, 'Of soup and love, the first is best.'" [19]

SHE-CRAB SOUP

Coastal Carolina and Georgia are famous for their She-Crab Soup. Originally this was not an extravagant gourmet *potage*, but a practical way of utilizing an abundance of sweet, meaty Atlantic Blue Crabs.

* * *

1/4 lb. butter
1 tbsp. flour
1 qt. milk
1/2 c. cream, whipped
2 c. white crabmeat and roe
Few drops onion juice
1/2 tsp. Worcestershire sauce
Mace, salt, and pepper to taste
4 tbsp. dry sherry
Whipped cream

In the top of a double boiler, melt butter and blend in flour. Add milk, cream, crabmeat, roe, and all seasonings, except sherry. Cook slowly 20 minutes over hot water. Pour 1/2 tbsp. warmed sherry into individual soup bowls. Add soup. Top each bowl with a dollop of whipped cream. Serve piping hot.

PART II

WELL-BREAD RECIPES

From an aristocratic soup, to yummy, ubiquitous biscuits, and other pleasing beadstuffs . . . .

JIFFY PB BISCUITS

Don't worry; the peanut butter taste isn't overpowering.

* * *

4 c. whole wheat flour
1 tbsp. baking powder
1/2 tsp. salt
1/3 c. molasses
3 tbsp. vegetable oil
2/3 c. peanut butter
2 1/2 c. (approx.) milk

    Mix dry ingredients. In a separate bowl, mix wet ingredients. Combine the two mixtures, using enough milk to make a moist, spoonable dough. Drop by spoonfuls onto a lightly greased baking sheet. Bake at 400° F. for approximately 12 minutes. (If the bottoms start getting brown too fast, turn the biscuits over.) -- Any of these recipes can be cut in half, or doubled.

COUNTRY HOME SCONES

    Healthful, with that good, earthy, grain flavor.

* * *

3 1/2 c. whole wheat flour
1/2 c. wheat germ
1 1/2 tsp. baking soda
1/2 tsp. cream of tartar
1/2 tsp. salt
2 tbsp. vegetable oil
2 tbsp. molasses
1 c. buttermilk or sour milk

    Combine the dry ingredients. In another container mix the liquids. Stir together the two mixtures, and then, using your hands, form two balls of dough. On a smooth surface press these balls down to flatten to a thickness of about 1 inch. Cut each round cake into 8 (or more) wedges. Place the wedges on lightly greased baking sheets and bake at 375° F. for approximately 10 minutes or until the bottoms have browned slightly. Turn over the wedges and bake about 5 minutes more. Incomparable served hot with butter.

Epitaph:

*I'd be content to have them utter,
"She was one who never scrimped on butter."*
                                        - Marcelene Cox

SWEET POTATO SHERRY SCONES

A little sweet and spicy, but not dessert-like.

* * *

4 c. whole wheat flour
2 tsp. baking powder
1/2 tsp. baking soda
1/4 tsp. salt
1 tbsp. cinnamon (optional)
1 tsp. allspice (optional)
3 - 4 tbsp. sugar
3 tbsp. vegetable oil
1/3 c. sherry
1 1/2 c. sweet potato, cooked and mashed
1 - 1 1/4 c. buttermilk or sour milk (approximately)

Mix the dry ingredients. In a separate bowl, mix the liquids. Combine the two mixtures, using enough milk to make a soft, yet kneadable dough. Form two balls of dough. On a lightly floured, flat surface pat each ball to a thickness of about an inch. Cut each disk into 8 wedges. Transfer to lightly greased baking sheets. Bake at 400° F. for around 12 minutes, turning over once during the baking time if the bottoms begin to get too brown.

LEMON-PARSLEY BISCUITS

I love lemon, so the juice and peel often slip into my cooking experiments . . . .

* * *

3 3/4 c. whole wheat flour
1 tbsp. baking powder
1/4 tsp. salt
3 tbsp. lemon peel, finely chopped
3 tbsp. lemon juice
3 tbsp. vegetable oil
1/3 c. fresh parsley, finely chopped
2 c. milk (approximately, for drop biscuits; less for rolled-out biscuits)

Combine the dry ingredients. In a large bowl mix lemon juice, oil, and parsley. Add milk and dry ingredients. For drop biscuits, plop large spoonfuls of batter onto lightly greased baking sheets. (For rolled-out biscuits, roll out and cut, then place on baking sheets.) Bake at 425° F. for about 12 minutes or until done, turning over the biscuits if the bottoms become too tan.

HE-MAN HERB BISCUITS

First we tried 'em with 1/4 c. onion; even he-man husband Henry said, "Too strong!" -- Two tablespoons onion work fine.

* * *

3 1/2 c. whole wheat flour
2 tsp. baking powder
1/2 tsp. salt
2 tbsp. onion, minced
1 tbsp. sugar
2 tsp. dry parsley
1/2 tsp. *each* garlic powder, dry basil, and dry sage
1/4 tsp. dry thyme
3 tbsp. vegetable oil
Milk

Combine the dry ingredients. In a separate bowl mix the oil and a cup of milk. Stir in the dry ingredients, adding sufficient milk to moisten. If you want to make rolled out biscuits, use less milk than if you plan to make drop biscuits. (Obviously I love drop biscuits because of their ease of preparation; plus, because they tend to be softer inside, you can get away with using little or no butter on them, and they still taste good and moist. -- These He-Man Herb Biscuits are even nice split open and drizzled with honey.) Back to the instructions: Form the type of biscuit you prefer, and situate them on a baking sheet. Bake at 425° F. for about 12 minutes. (If they are big they take a bit longer to cook, of course. You might wish to turn them over after about 10 minutes of baking time if you like them with a little crustier top and bottom, rather than the bottom crust being more crispy.)

FEEL-WELL WHEAT GERM BISCUITS

Some people would say that these biscuits are "healthy." That is grammatically incorrect. They are "*healthful*." -- (People and animals are *healthy*; foods aren't.) (The English major in me sometimes comes out . . . .)

* * *

3 c. whole wheat flour
1 c. wheat germ
1 heaping tbsp. baking powder
1/2 tsp. salt
1/4 c. vegetable oil
2 c. milk (approximately)

Mix dry ingredients. In a separate bowl, mix the wet ingredients. Combine and, if needed, add more milk to make a spoonable dough. Spoon mounds onto a lightly greased baking sheet and bake at 425° F. for 12-15 minutes.

MAYONNAISE SKILLET BREAD

Mayonnaise sneaks into the next bread recipe . . . . (Mayo is a handy short-cut ingredient in bread-making, because it adds fat and a little liquid plus tangy/creamy flavor all "in one fell swoop.")

* * *

2 c. self-rising flour
1 c. milk
1/3 c. mayonnaise
2 tbsp. vegetable oil
1 tsp. cornmeal

Stir together the flour, milk, and mayonnaise. Next pour the vegetable oil into a 10-inch cast-iron skillet, and heat in the oven at 400° F. for 4 minutes or until hot. Remove the skillet from the oven and sprinkle the inside bottom with the cornmeal. Spoon the batter into the skillet, and bake at 400° F. for 20-25 minutes or until browned lightly. (Oven temperatures can vary, despite what the oven thermometer reads, so be vigilant.)

WHEAT GERM BREAD STICKS

Be sure to serve these warm. They are much more delicious that way.

* * *

2 c. wheat germ
1 1/2 c. whole wheat flour
1/2 c. soy flour (or omit and use 1/2 c. whole wheat flour)
1/2 tsp. salt
1 1/2 c. (or more) milk
1/4 c. vegetable oil
1 tbsp. molasses or honey

Sesame seeds, caraway seeds, or poppy seeds (all optional)

Mix dry ingredients thoroughly. Add liquids. Mix. Form "sticks" or fat pencil shapes. Roll the bread sticks in the seeds, if desired. Bake at 350° F. for about 15 minutes.

SESAME SEED STICKS

Satisfying . . . .

* * *

1 1/2 c. whole wheat flour
1/2 c. cornmeal
1/2 tsp. baking soda
1/4 tsp. salt
1/2 tsp. paprika
2 tbsp. sesame seeds
2 tbsp. vegetable oil

1/2 c. plain yogurt
3/4 c. yellow or mozzarella cheese
1/2 - 3/4 c. milk

Mix the dry ingredients. In a different bowl, combine the remaining ingredients; and then stir together the two groups of ingredients, adding a bit more milk, if needed, to moisten. Work the dough into fat pencil shapes, and place on a large, lightly greased baking sheet. Bake at 400° F. for 12-15 minutes. (About midway through the baking time you may wish to roll each stick over so that they brown more uniformly.)

MAIZE 'N' MOZZARELLA DODGERS

These are yummy served hot out of the oven.

* * *

3 c. cornmeal
1/2 tsp. salt
1/2 tsp. garlic powder
1 1/2 c. boiling water (approximately)
1 1/2 c. mozzarella cheese (add last)

Mix the dry ingredients. Add boiling water to dry ingredients. When mixture has cooled some, add cheese and form into cornstick shapes. Bake on greased baking sheets at 375° F. for 10 minutes on one side and 5 minutes on other side. Serve warm. Makes approximately 2 - 3 dozen, depending on size.

TEFF, BUCKWHEAT, OR KAMUT CRACKERS

Lately I've been having a ball baking with "exotic" flours -- amaranth, kamut, millet, quinoa, teff, etc. I was "tossed into the briarpatch" of experimentation when a friend of mine, Adrienne Bishop, gave me several bags of uncommon flours and grains. What fun I've had testing new recipes!

* * *

3/4 c. teff, buckwheat, or kamut flour
1 1/4 c. whole wheat flour
1/4 tsp. salt
1/4 c. vegetable oil
1/2 c. plus 1/4 tsp. water

Mix the dry ingredients. In a separate bowl, stir together the wet ingredients. Combine. Roll out thinly. Cut into small squares (or whatever shape you like). Put on ungreased baking sheets and bake at 400° F. for approximately 8 minutes.

WHOLE WHEAT NORWEGIAN FLAT BREAD (LIKE CRACKERS)

These are excellent!

* * *

1/2 tsp. salt
1 tbsp. sugar
1 tbsp. butter

Cream together the above ingredients. Add:

2 c. whole wheat flour
2/3 c. milk

Roll out "flatly." Cut into small squares (or other shapes). Bake at 400° F. until done, turning once.

CHATHAM CARROT CRACKERS

Wholesome and colorful.

* * *

3/4 c. carrot, grated
2/3 c. water
2 tbsp. vegetable oil

1 1/2 c. oats
2/3 c. whole wheat flour
1/3 c. wheat germ
1 tbsp. sesame seed
1/2 tsp. garlic powder
1/4 tsp. salt

Combine the first 3 ingredients. Mix the dry ingredients and stir into the liquid mixture. Form a ball and roll out thinly. Place dough on baking sheets and score into small squares. Bake at 400° F. for about 8 minutes. When cool, break apart crackers.

"All American ladies should know how to clear-starch and iron: how to keep plate and glass: how to cook dainties: and, if they understand the making of bread and soup likewise, so much the better." [20]

- Harriet Martineau
Society in America (1836)

CORNFIELD BISCUITS

We like these a lot.

* * *

2 c. whole wheat flour
1 c. unbleached or all-purpose flour
1 c. cornmeal
1 tbsp. baking powder
1/2 tsp. salt
3 tbsp. vegetable oil
Milk

Mix dry ingredients. In a separate container, mix oil and 1 cup of milk. Stir together the two mixtures, adding more milk to make a kneadable dough. Knead briefly and pat out or roll out to a thickness of about 3/4-inch. Cut into square biscuits, or use a biscuit cutter to cut circles. Bake at 425° F. for 12-15 minutes. Serve hot with butter. (All the breads and crackers herein are best served warm.)

SWEET "YANKEE" CORN BREAD

The dose of sugar clues you in to the fact that this recipe comes from above the Mason-Dixon line.

* * *

1 c. cornmeal
1 c. flour
1/4 c. sugar
1 tsp. salt
4 tsp. baking powder
1 egg, beaten
1 c. milk
1/4 c. vegetable oil

Combine all ingredients in a medium bowl. Pour batter into a well greased 9-inch skillet or 9-inch glass baking dish. Bake in a preheated 425° F. oven for 20 to 30 minutes. Check for doneness.[21]

"A loaf of bread" the Walrus said, "Is what we chiefly need . . . ."[22]

- Lewis Carroll
Alice's Adventures in Wonderland

NO-SWEETENING YEAST BREAD

Sustaining . . . .

* * *

1 pkg. or 1 tbsp. baking yeast (or yeast cake)
3 c. warm milk, or half water and half milk (The use of milk produces a more flavorful, tender bread.)
2 tsp. salt
2 tbsp. wheat germ
4 1/2 c. whole wheat flour
3 c. (approx.) unbleached flour, bread flour, or all-purpose flour

Stir together the yeast and warm liquid. In about ten minutes, beat in the salt, wheat germ, and whole wheat flour. Gradually add enough light-colored flour to make a kneadable dough. On a floured, flat surface, knead the dough until smooth. Put in a covered bowl. Set in a warm-ish spot to rise. When it has doubled in bulk, punch down, and form two or three loaves. Put in greased bread pans (9x5-inch for two loaves; 8x4-inch for three), and cover lightly. Let rise until the dough is up over the sides of the pans. Bake at 375° F. for around 40 minutes (more or less, depending upon loaf size).

WHOLE-GRAIN GOODNESS YEAST BREAD

2 pkg. or 2 tbsp. baking yeast
1/2 c. warm water
1/4 c. honey and 2 tbsp. molasses *or* 1/3 c. honey total
2 c. warm milk
3 tbsp. vegetable oil or melted butter
2 - 2 1/2 tsp. salt
1/2 c. rye flour
1/4 c. wheat bran
1/4 c. wheat germ
3 c. whole wheat flour
3 c. (or more) unbleached flour, bread flour, or all-purpose flour
3/4 c. sunflower seeds

Combine the yeast and water. In a few minutes stir in the sweetener, warm milk, oil, salt, flours, and seeds. Knead well, adding more flour if necessary. Place in a bowl. Cover. Let rise in a warm place. When dough has risen well, punch down [WHAM!] and form two loaf shapes. Place in greased 9x5-inch bread pans. Allow to rise in a "cozy corner." When dough has mounded up nicely above the sides of the pans, bake in a preheated 375° F. oven until the loaves sound hollow when thumped -- about 40 minutes.

Note: You may increase the wheat bran and wheat germ to 1/2 c. each, and omit the sunflower seeds. (Of course, there are a zillion other ways you could vary this recipe. Have fun, experiment! A written recipe is just a guideline, a jumping off point for creativity.)

AUBREY'S BREAD

A recent happy memory for our family involves a dear old Louisiana friend and master of spontaneity, Aubrey C. Jenkins. He and several others showed up here unexpectedly at suppertime one night. ("Just passing through.") Thank goodness, that afternoon I had made a batch of this bread!

* * *

1 c. warm water
2 pkg. or 2 tbsp. baking yeast
2 tbsp. brown sugar, packed
1/4 c. vegetable oil
1 c. warm milk
1 c. warm water
1/4 c. molasses
1 scant tbsp. salt
1 c. rolled oats (old-fashioned, not quick)
1/4 c. cornmeal
1 c. rye flour
1 1/2 c. bread flour
1 1/2 c. whole wheat flour
3 - 4 c. unbleached or all-purpose flour, or as needed

Mix the warm water, yeast, and brown sugar. When the mixture bubbles, add the oil. Meanwhile combine the warm milk and water, the molasses, salt, oats, cornmeal, and rye flour. Add to the yeast mixture. Stir in the other flours. Knead, cover, and let rise.

Place in two greased 9x5-inch bread pans. Cover. Let rise. Bake at 350° F. around 40 minutes or until the loaves sound hollow when tapped.

"Nothing in the whole range of domestic life more affects the health and happiness of the family than the quality of its daily bread. With good bread, the plainest meal is a feast in itself; without it, the most elaborately prepared and elegantly served 'menu' is unsatisfactory." [23]

- Mary J. Lincoln
Mrs. Lincoln's Boston Cook Book, 1914

MEMORY BOOK COLONIAL BREAD

1/2 c. cornmeal
1/4 c. brown sugar, packed
3/4 tsp. salt
2 1/2 c. boiling water
1/4 c. vegetable oil

Mix. Cool. Add:

Approx. 4 1/2 - 5 c. unbleached flour, bread flour, or all-purpose flour
1 c. whole wheat flour
1/2 c. rye flour
1 pkg. or 1 tbsp. baking yeast

Knead and let rise according to directions for the preceding yeast breads. Form into two loaves. Let rise. Bake at 350° F. for 40 minutes.

YEASTY GRITS BREAD

This is really good. The grits are well-incorporated. In other words, they don't stick out like a sore thumb.

* * *

1 pkg. or 1 tbsp. baking yeast
2 c. warm water
1 tbsp. sugar
1 1/2 tsp. salt
2 c. cooked grits
1 tbsp. vegetable oil
1 c. whole wheat flour
5 - 6 c. unbleached flour, bread flour, or all-purpose flour

Combine the yeast, warm water, and sugar. When it bubbles, add the salt, grits, and oil. Work the mixture into a smooth liquid (no lumps of grits). Stir in the whole wheat flour, and enough white flour to make a soft, yet workable dough. Knead well, and then let the covered dough rise in a warm place for an hour. Punch down and shape into two loaves. Place in two 9x5-inch greased loaf pans. Let rise until the bread is well over the sides of the bread pans. Bake at 375° F. for 35-45 minutes.

NO-KNEAD CASSEROLE BREAD

No sore muscles from kneading! (A real possibility for inexperienced yeast bread makers or frail bakers.)

* * *

1 pkg. or 1 tbsp. baking yeast
2/3 c. warm water
2 tbsp. sugar
1 c. whole wheat flour
1 1/2 c. unbleached flour, bread flour, or all-purpose flour
1 tsp. salt
2 tbsp. vegetable oil
2/3 c. milk
1 egg

Dissolve yeast and sugar in water, in a small bowl. Put 1 c. whole wheat flour and salt in a large bowl. Add oil, milk, egg and yeast/sugar/water. Stir until moistened. Beat with electric mixer for 3 minutes at low speed. Stir in by hand 1 1/2 c. white flour to make a stiff batter (this will be "batter" not "dough"). Cover loosely and let rise until doubled in size. Stir down, and pour into a greased 8-inch casserole dish (do not knead). Cover casserole dish loosely. Let rise 30-40 minutes. Place in *cold* oven and bake at 375° F. for 35-40 minutes.

BATTER-UP OATMEAL BREAD (NO-KNEAD)

2 pkgs. or 2 tbsp. baking yeast
2 1/4 c. warm water
1 tbsp. vegetable oil
1/4 c. molasses
1 c. quick oats

1 tsp. salt
2 c. whole wheat flour
About 2 c. unbleached flour, bread flour, or all-purpose flour

Stir together the first five ingredients. When the mixture bubbles, add the salt and gradually beat the flour into the batter. Use only enough to create a stiff dough that leaves the sides of the bowl. Loosely cover the bowl; let dough rise in a warm area until doubled, about 1 hour. Stir down the dough, and divide into two parts. Place the dough in two well-greased, shallow casserole dishes. With greased fingers, turn each glob of dough over to grease the top. Pat into rounded hump shapes. Cover loosely with two light-weight, clean kitchen towels. In an hour, or when the dough has risen nicely, bake at 350° F. for about 40 minutes, or until the loaves sound hollow if tapped. If you like, rub the tops with butter or margarine. Serve immediately, slicing the bread and serving it from the casserole dish right at the table (our informal way), or allow the bread to cool on wire racks before removing to serve later.

DILLY CASSEROLE BREAD

This recipe was winner of the 1960 Pillsbury $25,000 prize.

* * *

1 pkg. or 1 tbsp. baking yeast
1/4 c. warm water
1 c. cottage cheese, heated to lukewarm
2 tbsp. sugar
1 tbsp. instant minced onion
1 tbsp. butter
2 tsp. dill seed
1 tsp. salt
1/4 tsp. baking soda
1 egg, unbeaten
2 1/4 c. (or more) unbleached flour, bread flour, or all-purpose flour

Soften yeast in water and add to other ingredients. Add flour to form stiff dough, beating well after each addition. Cover; let stand in a warm place (85-90° F.) until light and doubled in size (50-60 minutes). Stir down dough. Turn into a well-greased 8-inch casserole dish (2 quarts). Let rise 30-40 minutes until light. Bake at 350° F. 40 or 50 minutes until golden brown. Brush with soft butter for a shiny crust. Makes one round loaf.

MY HONEY'S FRENCH BREAD

1 pkg. or 1 tbsp. baking yeast
2 c. warm water
2 tbsp. honey
1 tsp. salt
2 c. whole wheat flour
3 c. (more or less) unbleached flour, bread flour, or all-purpose flour

    Combine yeast, water, and honey. When the yeast is lively (activated and bubbly) add the salt and whole wheat flour. Stir well. In a big bowl, stir together that mixture and enough white flour to make a workable dough. Knead well. Place the ball of dough in a greased bowl. Cover. Let rise in a warm place until doubled in bulk. Punch down. Form two long baguette-like shapes and place on a lightly greased baking sheet. Make a few diagonal cuts along the tops of the loaves. Cover, let rise, then bake in a preheated 375° F. oven for 20-25 minutes, or until golden on top.

PANE DI CAMPAGNA
(HEARTY COUNTRY LOAF)

    This European-style loaf will make any soup taste better. -- Enjoy!

* * *

2 pkg. or 2 tbsp. baking yeast
1/3 c. warm water
Pinch of sugar
1 1/3 c. warm water
1/4 c. wheat bran
3 c. unbleached flour, bread flour, or all-purpose flour
1 tsp. salt

2 tbsp. wheat bran

    Dissolve the yeast in the 1/3 c. warm water with the pinch of sugar. When it is bubbly, add the 1 1/3 c. warm water, the bran, and the salt. Gradually add flour, forming a kneadable, yet slightly sticky dough. Knead. Put in a greased bowl. Let rise in a warm place. When doubled, punch down, form a ball and roll it in the 2 tbsp. bran. Flatten to a thick disk shape in a 10-inch pie plate. Cover. Let rise. Bake at 425° F. for around 30 minutes.

* * * * * * * * * * * * *

Last night we were at Mom's for dinner (no soup, you understand, having read about Mom . . .). After eating, I complimented her on the meal, and she demurred, saying how simple the food was. I replied that we **like** non-threatening food. -- It is nice to be confident that nothing will be so spicy hot that you'll have to gulp water, or so exotic that you have to ask what it is, or so unhealthful that you feel guilty about abusing your body.

The recipes in this book are **comfortable**. Even today, with the book complete, we had Commemorative Voyager Stew and cornmeal scones for lunch. In fact, I serve soup at least once and often twice a week. As William Byrd II of colonial Virginia wrote about an " . . . excellent soupe": "It never cloy'd, no more than Engaging Wife wou'd do, by being a Constant Dish." [24]

* * * * * * * * * * * * *

NOTES

[1] Margaret Jaworski, "Circle This," *Family Circle*, Feb. 1, 1990, p. 9.

[2] Sheila Hibben, *The National Cookbook: A Kitchen Americana*, Harper & Brothers Publishers, New York, 1932, p. x.

[3] Julee Rosso and Sheila Lukins, *The Silver Palate Cookbook*, Workman Publishing, New York, 1982, p. 44, quote attributed to "Kitchen Graffitti."

[4] Isabella Beeton, *The Book of Household Management*, S. O. Beeton, London, 1861, p. 47.

[5] Recipe courtesy Epps Perrow, Hurt, VA.

[6] Lewis Carroll, *Alice in Wonderland and Through the Looking-Glass*, reprinted by E. P. Dutton & Co., Inc., New York, 1954, p. 91.

[7] Niccolo de Quattrociocchi, *Love and Dishes*, The Bobbs-Merrill Co., New York, 1950, p. 175.

[8] Recipe courtesy Bea Lilly, Hammond, LA.

[9] Recipe courtesy Marcelle Bienvenu, St. Martinville, LA.

[10] J. Berjane, *French Dishes for English Tables: Soups & Potages, Hor D'Oeuvre, Salads*, Frederick Warne & Co., Ltd., New York, 1931, p. 1.

[11] Alice Cooke Brown, *Early American Herb Recipes*, Charles E. Tuttle, Co. Inc./Bonanza Books, New York, 1966, p. 96, quoting from *Young Housekeeper's Friend*, 1846.

[12] June Platt, *June Platt's Plain and Fancy Cookbook*, Houghton Mifflin Co., Boston, 1941, p. 54.

[13] Frances Parkinson Keyes, "Spécialités De La Maison," *Town & Country*, Feb. 1958, Hearst Corp., New York, p. 134.

[14] Hibben, p. 42.

[15] Recipe courtesy Louisiana Seafood Promotion & Marketing Board, New Orleans, LA.

[16] Ibid.

[17] Recipe courtesy Evelyn Revertiga, Honfleur Restaurant, Hôtel Provincial, New Orleans, LA.

[18] Rosso and Lukins, p. 51.

[19] Phillip Stephen Schulz, *As American As Apple Pie*, Simon and Schuster, New York, 1990, p. 169.

[20] Betty Fussell, *Masters of American Cookery*, Times Books, New York, 1983, p. 54.

[21] Recipe courtesy Fowler's Mill, Cardon, OH.

[22] Carroll, p. 160.

[23] Mary J. Lincoln, *Mrs. Lincoln's Boston Cook Book: What to do and What not to do in Cooking*, Rev. Ed., Little, Brown, and Co., Boston, 1914, p. 36.

[24] William Byrd, *The Dividing Line*, 1728, reprinted in John Spencer Bassett, ed., *The Writings of "Colonel William Byrd of Westover in Virginia Esqr.,"* Doubleday, Page, & Co., New York, 1901, p. 128.